Snow House

BRIAN SWANN

Snow House

Lena-Miles Wever Todd Poetry Series
PLEIADES PRESS
Warrensburg, Missouri
& Rock Hill, South Carolina

ISBN 0-8071-3167-9

Published by Pleiades Press
Department of English & Philosophy
Central Missouri State University
Warrensburg, Missouri 64093
&
Department of English
Winthrop University
Rock Hill, South Carolina 29733

Distributed by Louisiana State University Press

2 4 6 8 9 7 5 3 1
First Pleiades Press Printing, 2006

Cover painting: © Brian Swann
Cover design by Joy Katz & Kevin Prufer

Many of these poems appeared previously in *Agni, American Scholar, Anthropology and Humanism, Antioch Review, Conjunctions, CrazyHorse, International Quarterly, Iowa Review, ISLE, Massachussetts Review, Midwest Quarterly, New England Review, The New Republic, North American Review, Notre Dame Review, Ploughshares, Poetry East, Queen's Quarterly, Raritan, Seneca Review, Sewanee Review, Southern Review, Southwest Review, Stand, Verse,* and *Yale Review*. "The Necessary Angel" appeared in *September 11, 2001,* ed. William Heyen (Etruscan Press, 2002). "Naked" first appeared in *The Georgia Review.* "Egg" and "Manitu Bay" first appeared in *Poetry.*

This book is for Roberta,
as always, with love.

CONTENTS

Fractals—

Natura Naturans—

i
Fractals

Naked

Here springs spurt, over and over,
pulsing and arcing, the same water
shifting its weight in some sort of balance,
rebuff and reception, responding to hidden stirrings
where the land is parchment and sand
blows like fire. Survivors have come
to terms with it. A wildcat walks to
the water's edge, articulate and thin,
a fox barks and scours. But this is not
a landscape. This is a mark I've made
to keep the story straight, reminding me
that plots are variations on a song
that begins and ends. There are others.
For instance, the moon's so lovely
the sky turns hollow around her over
fields where foals have arrived, ecstatic,
and bees plunder. All this I see in the moment:
everything naked and empty as balloons,
filled with dazzlement, gadding about
blended and particular, immense and rich.
I have nowhere else to go. I have
nothing else to say or do. Words are my
furious twin turning about like that
week-old calf making an inventory
of his muscles. In these clearest mornings
is no waste, no indifference. Here I am
proving unprovable, making everything
I've lived by, the guilty weave, a swarm
shattering with flight, here and there.
I had no parents, no family or place,
and now just stories. They are knackery,
but I can't stop. In another I start taking

on rocks and arcs, thread and pulp.
The universe is spinning out bubbles,
hypnotic with tow and undertow, pleasure
so immense my knees shake and I live between
my name and galaxies where the catalpa is
all foam and function, the air silver saxophone
and barely syntax, where solitude flashes
in a field of purple thyme, and from this
everything falls naked and touch is
like a waterfall that never stops, a place
to sit, feel pebbles slippery and wet, and
the story of all this redundant and necessary.

Fractals

We cannot claim it wants us,
  the wind at dawn. Yet windows & walls
are understood now in a different way
  & dimensions come uncluttered,
flowering within flowers.
  There is no time to think;
thoughts gather as weather until
  contents make the container.
Everywhere starts clapping & gliding.
  Trees give up a branch here & there.
The power in the world releases itself
  & the clicking of childhood grows &
grows before it blows out the barn door
  & children burst out laughing,
in tow & towing, ripening as they run,
  some pretending to be their favorite
flower, fruit or animal, others
  still deep in mirrors mirroring
every action, their voices
  stand clear, & from distances call out
to come to them where the wind,
  now wide-hipped, fullthroated,
shares the world with birds, spoons out
  the sun's yolk, wrestles in streams
with currents, starts fires where twigs
  flare like broken bones across each other.
Whatever comes near them lights up
  forever. Oh, the rush of indomitable unities
that have to be there & if they are
  will never let you starve.

Artificer

From windwrought headland I watch
   the water break into harsh sparks,
lit and relit from inside, out and out,
   echelon on echelon of rough
estuary lace, salt and sweet running
   together over and under, past islet
and lighthouse, everything at stake,
   guttering down then flaring up again
holding up weather and wearing gulls,
   a waking mind, always waking, fully awake,
leaning in on something, piling up in the distance
   more distance beyond itself in a constant quarrel
I resolve in the shape I call music.

Manitu Bay

The scraps, bright, all of them,
these small birds, as if torn from the sun
now bloody-mouthed, then a broken
line moving closer, brant—no,
blue geese, and in synapses all round
swamp-sparrows, as blades of light
push in till the last one takes over
so masks drop from stones and
on the headland windowpanes
are morning swollen and a wave curves
like gravel along the long bay
where no hull moves so it all starts
to look a little contrived, as if the boats
had gone out to sea on cue, and hidden.
Here you find yourself shattered at a thousand points,
flashing like crabs, an leg here, a claw
there, and eyes everywhere.

Snow House:
ena qanikcaq

"A Yupik word is not merely a static construct but may approach a dynamic sentence in microcosm"

—Osahito Miyaoka

"Man is…unshielded"

—Martin Heidegger

Sharp edges, rounded off to the
  nearest curve, how many worlds
can you make at random, if
  random is the world seen
in extremis, whole sentences strung
  out, making sense of whatever
each lands on, taking from it,
  giving. Parts of this speech are
everywhere, in flocks and little songs,
  a wild chirping in cochlea and
cloud. And from this houses are made,
  all the same and all different.
Lapidary but loose in syntax it covers
  everything, making itself up as it
goes along, as it falls, loosening
  the land, and tightening it up,
blown this way and that by gust
  and gale, only to pile up and link
with starry burrs on a continent
  of give-back, a whole whirling
world of joists and angles linking
  and renewing, unlike anything and
like everything, more and more itself,
  glass that drops over you
so you shine brighter out.

Wittgenstein's Screw

The calendar moves by degrees.
   Someone's finger is pointing at the rain,
at gulls in gray dunes that float up
   into their inverse likeness. There they hover
as torn up clouds over beaches drifting
   with the tide, dancing with it, draping
themselves over so they seem unmoving.
   Then I see a heron by the inlet.
He stands, one thing, unmoved, as if
   cut out from whatever had stood there
before him, exactly filling his space
   so nothing is left over, scissored out
of gray blue sky and cloud, gray blue water
   so the longer you look the more he
disappears until at last what you thought
   some sort of finality, some definitive shape,
is gone, and you look right through to sky
   and water and beyond to gulls marking dunes
like punctuation until they too are released
   into water and cloud, and the ripe rain is turning
and moving straight at you as if it is something,
   and the sky moves on, turning like
Wittgenstein's screw that turns without moving
   any part of the mechanism to which it is attached.

On Inhabiting a Tree

"All our roads go nowhere"

—Josephine Miles

Then, maps were the body,
  chanting a mimetic inventory.
Its breath climbed and spoke from trees.
  Everything was afflatus, and so moved,
until everything became mouth, an aching jaw
  chewing on light like leather. What
had been light became tinfoil. A trellis
  of scrollwork grew from the tree which
shivered and lodged. Its leaves became
  letters, its bark books, its birds notes.
Its clouds stuck, edges spinning on
  "but," "however," "in the event that,"
"none—" and "nevertheless," quoting themselves
  in "an endless detour."

The Shield of Achilles

On it I engrave another scene in which
  I gave them what they wanted, "things
as they are," although it was not mine to give.
  They'd guessed that much, having seen through
my disguise and noticed my limp. They'd take it
  all the same, they said. You never know.
But when they left they didn't—by then I had confessed
  that all I do is forge whatever's needed
with whatever comes to hand, stick things where
  they make or don't make sense, such as here
and now where birds rise over the river's mouth
  then sweep above pines, flexed, looking to be
understood the way the world once was, which
  I still try to do, so that in that seagull's eye
I'd turn vast and burn into things, making something
  that will eventually unmake itself, and so on.
I try a phrase to stamp it into yet another shape
  but something flashes from it like a file of fire ants
and I follow, heading to where more seabirds have returned
  to sit on an old wreck, staring at the sky as if
it was something on its own, not theirs. Then
  something spooks them and they take off into the curve
of the horizon I blow on until a flame erupts that,
  passing, leaves black streaks on clouds and along
the sides of this house like the ocean's mark when it
  withdraws to flow around the edge of the shield which is
the world which could be you but isn't, ever, quite.

Birds in the Woods

Silence is involved in itself as
loads of light float down white
as the flames that lighted on
the disciples with the gift
of tongues. Just after dawn,
I'm waiting for sleep to unravel
just enough so I can speak
in a voice still not mine, one
perhaps like the carpenter's
down the road who makes
models that may not look
like much you recognize,
but work. What does it take
to scrap the patterns and
start again? There are things
I know but have never seen
or heard, syllables self-effacing,
interlocking but not quite
consistent, solid, but not quite
there. I like it when culverts
trail after the streams they're
built to contain; when after
storms great cords of water
interweave, or get torn apart
again but you wouldn't know it.
It could be the same thing,
forces forming and reforming.
When the time comes I'd
like to be something like that.
Things will continue to wear
themselves out, but still
be standing. Birds will sing
in the woods but the woods
will be gone.

ii
Natura Naturans

Coyote

neat in brown & gray, boater at an angle
on his head, airing his quiff, coming to consume
my deckchairs & gardening equipment, pick my moonflowers
& my wife, rolling down my path like water
until, seeing me, the turn & conflagration of his tail
dries him up at once. That spring, I'd found traces
of transcendence along that path, poked it with a stick
to see what went into it. But now—the *Ding an sich!*
Or was it? Like Red Riding Hood with my blueberry basket
on my arm, I continued on my way, unsure of what
I'd seen. Perhaps I'd read too much. I moved
cautiously out into my field that was now mine
no more, flowing down south-east like the alluvial silt
it once was, until a quick stir in the grass almost
made me jump into my basket, go with the flow.
I closed my eyes. When I opened them—nothing. Just
wooded mountains, empty path, blueberries like little bells
ringing right & left, pines counting the days &
whispering, & over all wind sounding the All Clear,
just like when I was a kid & the sirens signalled the
temporary end to doodlebug & shrapnel. So, all clear
on a dog-day afternoon, keys falling back to minor,
I settled down to a domestic picking. But as I moved
from patch to patch I felt little flames flicker &
a smell like glass flowed in from clumps of willowherb
& hardhack. I stood, waiting to hear, perhaps,
a halleluia yodel from the other side of the wall &
scatter the cows, set off the dogs, make the farmer
look up in my direction & go get his shotgun. But
nothing. So I climbed the wall. Was I the only one
could smell the smoke, feel the rush of wind, see
a shadow like a gunshot? And then I heard
a deeper breath. Was that me breathing, an air so cool

& local I wouldn't need to speak for some time?
A tree flared, & the blue sky showed a white half-moon
with half a crazy gray face in it as if the rest
of the body was too light to stay. Then, way off in a
dark stand of spruce & hemlock a yelp, a clatter,
a hawk, a gargle. Suddenly, a whole band was up there,
tuning up, then slowly sliding into a kind of
celestial circular breathing, all held together by
a swooping tenor sax. They ran through a few numbers,
stumbled, struggled, collapsed, ending in a silence
like the sound after the toilet has finished flushing,
the tank full, fresh water settled. And all the birds
started up again like I'd never heard before.

Natura Naturans

She, or he, appears from nowhere & disappears
back into it down burrows I can see—in flowerbeds,
under lawnchairs, among vegetables—& others I can't.
When seasons change, she travels to the other side
of the house to dig deeper, closer, no doubt,
to the basement's warmer wall & just below our bed
on the ground-floor where, in storm, in snow,
I imagine I can hear her deep breathing all winter,
her head & ours a few sleeping inches apart, maybe
sharing dreams, chasing, being chased, give & take.
I have been careful not to tame her (not that I could).
But now, a day before my birthday, I've left an extra
handful of seeds on the steps where she is sitting
like a Buddha back on her haunches, holding one
as if it were a gold piece, testing the edges
with her teeth before taking it inside where it glows
through her flanks flashing with the rapid heartbeats
I'm sure I can hear over the quick cracking of shells.
Fragments cling to whiskers trembling like
sensitive thoughts. As I watch while she stuffs her cheeks
I whisper pet names, Chippy, Honey, Squirt. I call her
Larry Adler in a riff of puffed cheeks, or tell her
she's a streamliner with stripes like the Coronation Scot
I got for my twelfth birthday. Then, when I stop,
pouches filled to bursting, she stops too, scratches,
washes her face, turns, &, leaving not a crumb behind,
vanishes into her own alien life.
When she doesn't return,
I leave too, go about my day, another one piling up
in my anxious store. From time to time I try to picture
that life underground or dashing about in inaccessible places,
or even where I'd seen her once, dozing at the tip
of a bouncing pine-branch high up, like a cabin-boy
in a crow's nest.

That evening, dishes washed & stacked
above well-stocked cupboards, sitting across from my wife
who's already deep in a book, I look up from skimming mine
& wonder what she's thinking. The setting sun of late summer
is slipping through loose slats in the blinds onto her face.
Two white lines go over & under her sharp jet-black
irisless eyes. A gray line runs through & across her cheeks.
Her face slopes to a point of a tiny black nose.
While I stare, she has started to say something,
but what falls to the floorboards are little crunching sounds,
so small I can scarcely make them out,
though I try to chase & catch each one.

Tamias Striatus Poetics

"The poem is a sort of animal"
—Ted Hughes

I give him words to tell me who he is.
He gives them back, begins a visual discourse
on invisibility, gunning by me a film in snippets &

jump-shots, starring him. Light flashes everywhere.
But you can still make out frames that form a sequence,
though there are deep lacunae only he can leap

as a kind of semiotic stuntman—I guess it's him, though
it could be a series of doubles (impossible to know).
There—in that shot he's signifying a signified, so

in what follows he's multiple as the seeds he collects
like mnemonics. There, off he goes again, but now in a
series of silent sequences subtitled: "The Vital Nothing,"

"The Plump Filling," "The Cake of Soap," "The Full Stop,"
&, dramatically, "Tamias Striatus Meets Pale Ramon."
He's starting to blur like a piece of stained air, or

something identical. But to what? Himself? He cuts a
dashing solipsism, so comparisons are useless. Now he's
riding a fast vehicle. He *is* a vehicle. But of what?

Himself? Here we go again.... I'm about to call him accident
& let it go at that, but suddenly a small yet purposeful charge
goes off & something claps shut after itself, closing me out.

All I can hear is a series of fingersnaps, fragments of old songs,
theatrical effects that burrow into worlds & then pop up again,
now here, now there, more believable the more you believe.

Clearly, he's an idea whose time has come & gone almost
   in the same instant, an ironic reading that can't quite
cancel itself out. So this reader's response is to have him stay

   just as he is, whatever that is, in that moment when I can say
he's there, because as soon as I say he isn't he jumps out
   of my head, skitters off fingertips, skirrs just behind my heels,

& off we go again. He's turning me inside out, in circles, stripping
   my defenses. He's—*wait! There he is! He's there!* What you see is
what you get. But what have I seen? Sometimes you can think

  too much. I give in. He knocks me out.

Chipmunk

If, as Kit Smart said, toads have compensation
  for being toads, "since there are stones whose
constituent particles are toads," this particular
  Algonquian helps constitute a granite range
whose high inflections interweave. He flows
  between subject and object, neither and both.
He is, as the linguists say, non-configurational,
  and like the wind up there no one can tell
whence he came or where he goes. He's all
  action, all tiny jerks whose frames overlap
so quick they almost look seamless, impulses
  received and renewed just about at the
same time and at the same fast speed but
  as if that is too slow and he could go faster
if he really tried. Impulse and impulse,
  each thought an impulse tried successfully
many times over. Try saying him.
  Try thinking him with no words.

A Parable

I got up early and went out
into air caught between multiples
of glare, uneven, shatter-proof, un-
fettered. I could have been in
the paleolithic. Flowers rang
the mountainside, cavalier bells,
a non-event, not intended to be
seen or heard. But all things work
to their opposite. I saw and heard,
and could have stayed, but back
I went to the workaday neolithic
to dig and delve, and in my garden
give cucurbites of all kinds one
last chance. Forth I went again,
already some twenty bucks in the hole
to chipmunk familiars I'd named
Mary, Mark, Ruth and John. And again,
almost before I'd planted the seeds
in soil pitted with lilliput craters they'd
dug them up. And so, as promised,
I quit. But not them. On they dug,
even if what they searched for was
no longer there. There was collateral
damage, with Eden now the wasteland,
a monument to the principle:
what once was shall be again.

The Opening

The squirrel has sworn to keep, not give away.
I look past the birdfeeder to where the early sun's
a wafer, thin and furious, gradually becoming aware
of yellow, one tone, all around, one dandelion note
made up of many, that rises from the ground,
one bright note that could be a bull's snort,
a clink of coin from a far country brought here
for trade. There is no map. There is no score.
Then my eyes go out of focus and what
had been a fugue becomes a flood, something
that warms the flesh and opens the hand,
makes distance a still center spreading out
to where pines break and climb the mountains'
decreasing blue and mist, an opening
like a clear pool, the center me.

Skunk Poem

A white V, a minor flight of geese
  who live close to the ground and eat gravel—
no, it's him, here he comes again, though
  it's the first time I've actually seen him,
bobbling his walk as if it was hot, cooled
  by his ostrich tail, flowing at a constant speed,
his black nose alert as ants. He knows where
  he's headed—straight up the drive in his
low-slung Packard and into the garage
  for whatever fuel we've left, mostly
just the scent of garbage. But this time
  it's down. Without missing a beat
he turns and steers into the huckleberries
  then up into the small pines and—
gone. But when I look up, there he is,
  floating straight north, leaving the rest of him
to some subtle place in the mind, not missing
  a beat at cloudbank or windgust.
There are not many poems about skunks.
  Even their name is used against them.
 But they are not as earthbound
  as we make out. Few things are.

Old Squaw

Narrow rooftops live out
  broken sentences. Along the
slick road a snarl of wind.
  The steep avenue's a
cable taking something
  in tow—the March sun
at its frayed end.
  Rain's held off, so
a bride can sleep, floating
  above those roofs all
veil and silk—no,
  pigeons, no, ducks,
old squaw? Not a line
  or v but wheeling over
this rusting bridge that
  spans a canal once stream,
turning as one, with nowhere
  home but as if everywhere
was, choosing after
  tilt and veer, flex from
the hip, flashing white bellies
  as they sweep and flow
over my car, and I go out
  the window with a heave
of wordless love that could
  still save me, face to face,
as they lock into their purpose,
  going.

Ordinary

"The world is spirit; it can't be worked on"

—Lao Tzu

Today, everything has lived for ever.... From
  unclouded space, slowly, white laundry, a wake
coming back—geese
  picking up the flyway north,
dropping dead skin I catch on my tongue.
  Then air opens wider to wild swans,
each soul at that height male nor female,
  fixing the clock at one sweet point whose focus
is emptiness, whose every wingbeat's a sail
  making the land move & agree in an old tongue
spoken fresh; bodiless in bodies of shadow &
  countershadow that grows from the sky
down & earth up, substance as spirit,
  annunciation as ordinary.

Lightning-Flash-Being

Hunched over controls, engine like fingers
running through a comb, a bolt of Blakean delight
aiming straight at Urizen, voice the lightning's voice, electric,
sun emblazoned on each wing, tailfins forked like antennas
to catch and amplify the cosmos, multi-colored prayer-sticks
stuck in his hair.... He balks, almost out. Fuels up again
to take it out on air, chocks away, a backflip à la Olga—he drives
as if driven by some deep-seated slight, real or imagined,
dropping color like foil to elude eyes, shooting off, buzzing
himself in glass, chasing himself away, poking his nose
into any business, even mine, on the porch before seven,
a smear of sun on my head that's some sweet thought
waiting for inspection and probe from this extraterrestrial
who's just crossed the solar system & is now climbing vertically,
dropping at breakneck speed, then shooting off
at ninety degrees since g-forces don't apply
in this deep New Mexico sky as hospitable to
flying saucers as hummingbirds—though the former
have crashed here and their baby-faced dead
carted off for inspection, *these* guys never crash,
their technology more advanced, making every color
count, created out of blank by minds that split
the time/space continuum. However, if one ever does
come down, and if someone does step out alive,
you can bet he won't have goggle-eyes and skin like wax. No—
nose long as a flute, pack on his back full of who knows
what wonders; clad not in dull aluminum but a sun-suit
dazzling to the eye, with something to say that will
amaze us, not just for what he has to tell,
but the way in which he tells it.

The Owl

I imagine he's sitting nearby
like a Sufi on a roof, hollow-eyed,
intense, burning at midnight.
Something snaps. He has learned
the art of breaking & being broken.
His call is naked as a needle, sharp
as images he sorts from afterimages,
arranging them like flames. In the pines
he echoes off stone walls, blue snow.
Bones turn beautiful under his gaze.
His voice makes you want to quit
your job & go somewhere far away
that may never have existed,
but you want it, for what doesn't
exist can exist always. Then
he is just his sound fading,
calling as if only to himself,
waiting if he answers, & moves on,
perhaps trying to catch up.
When he's gone you don't know
he's gone, or if he was ever there.

The Owl: Part II

I once wrote a poem about this owl.
Well, not really an owl. That's
the sadness of poems. They're always
about something else. So, this owl
did various things that amounted to
very little, but it was enough. He
flew a bit, hooted, disappeared.
It was at night, so what could I know?
What could I know he knew?
I tried to find out. He could have been
anything. I suppose it could have been
my mother up there, or my father, yes,
a ghost. So—there, it just hooted!
But I'm not falling for the same trick again.
Wherever we go we know we've been
before. There is no center to this forest.
And the owl is there, moving as I move.
He might as well be a parrot in a cage,
not even aware he's in a cage. And that's
you, feeding him lines he feeds you back.
Would he rather be himself? Would you?

The Swan

In the blackness you can hear
   light pushing up. Sky throws
off stars. Stranded, they pause,
   then pass. The first swans
fly in from the north, clear as
   a constellation. Soon streams
are cascading cicadas spurting
   and shattering. A fragrance
opens and hides. Day spreads
   until there is no distinction
between things. I memorize
   the swans so they fill
this and other skies for a while
   before falling back into
the cold they came from.

Dark Horizons

Osprey at sundown to the left of a
  cool moon stretching out into a sky
caked dirt-hard over drowned farms & homes,
  flowing in air that drives past the risk
of sounds & a man looking up laughs
  like a cavern under snow & the path
he's on turns again in a manner so quiet
  he does not remember it turning.
The bird blows out of the sun's last draft
  & the man calls out his name like a
defense mechanism. It hovers while he
  stands in mud & twigs like busted springs
& looks up again before more rain drives his
  footprints down beyond words where
inchoate life crinkles like cellophane
  & breaks off into new impulses whose
intensity he can only guess at, what is
  being laid down, what winds are blowing,
what is rushing over rocks on dark horizons....

First Wood Thrush

"Darkling I listen…"

—John Keats

It's a long time, but from the black stalk cut across
  by chickadee sharps he doesn't spare you.
He's back, fast falling waters, lost voices, swamps & forests,
  a continent of flickering stars. In this mountain mist
pretending it isn't here he lights the maples' new red tips.
  Betraying the dead he again opens poor bones.
And he has started to suffer again, calling in aboriginal stillness
  so ghosts fly out of dead leaves all of whose echoes are the same.
In lifelines that never change he ensures they don't.
  If his tongue casts shadows, the threads wind & rewind,
spools of autonomy & dependence, taunting & disappearing,
  hiding in open air. His fiction draws on silence
whose origins could have been a scream
  but are now notes he scatters, whatever he is or has been,
wherever, holding it all together with strings
  of ventriloqual beads, making everything adjacent.
But it's not. It is always just off the fingertips,
  just beyond course or current, something
at a tangent, only for a while keeping off the awful irremediable dead.

Crow

Walking through the night of stinging plants,
the fading pen-light in my hand the only pathfinder,
I stumble among rocks where roots twist
and grip. The light dies. I push deeper
where snow begins, caked as if it never melted.
Here the sap will not run, and yet I feel
the land flowing away like shadows of fish
on the lake bottom. I hear the nighthawk
moving away from the edges of fire-scoured
clearings, and realize I have been here before,
when crows were hunting crickets in the grass,
heads just showing like loons carved among waves.
Exhausted, I gather pine boughs, lie under
the dull percussion of the moon. From where
a large star is caught in the top of a
giant hemlock, an owl calls, again and again.
I sleep—gasp for breath as a blue carp
rises to the air that floats barely a
handbreadth over my head. I wake to a crow
on my hand glowing so fresh sharp glass
could not cut it. It focuses the world
into something clear and hard, cold
and close to me.

Egg

"We are in the position of defining myth by the shape of its absence."
—Sean Kane, *Wisdom of the Mythtellers*

The bluebird's cold mistimed egg
fetched up from the one-legged
box after the pair had left for
points south & unknown (never,
as it turned out, to return) I
renested in the half-geode by
the windowsill where it gleamed
&, months becoming years, seemed
about to last forever, grow more
consistent with itself, holding its pure
blue firmament up over what by now
was nothing, till one January day, snow
melting to a fast flood,
I blew it softly onto my palm so I could
hold its cerulean up against new sky,
home against home, where it lay
weightless & delicate as the Xmas ornament
we'd just put away, but when I went
to roll it gently back onto its bed,
& leave it there, I saw a thread,
a crack, another, watched it sink in
slowly on itself, shard on shard collapsing
from my touch & breath, relaxing
into the shape of its absence

Impressions

"The gods who were once there, return only at the right times. . . ."

—Martin Heidegger, *Poetry, Language, Thought*

Large flat stones I'd laid as a path tossed aside,
scattered like book leaves. Four huge deep prints
plumb in the middle of the garden, each foot lifted
over plants into soft earth. And nothing else. No way in,
none out, like some cartoon. Certainly there used to be
gods here, presences that filled our expectations.
But now it comes out wrong, as if it's all made up.
And of course it is: counter and countershadow,
something intractable not quite evading the eye,
like the fading pressure of intensity, like the heart itself,
like anything we thread together and which threads us,
rhythms that mean each other, syllables that fit
whatever they can, where they can. Night first,
then morning fitted into these prints that show
and are lost where light hits or doesn't. From earth
to trees to sky then anywhere you have to create
proof for a story that will eventually come
face to face with you and find words to recognize
itself, each one leaving an impression, adding up
to itself, to you, keeping fresh, keeping true.

The Ironic Bears

There are few bears here, but
   what there are share their
unusual sense of things. So when
   you see they're dancing on the lawn,
flatfooted and slobbery, pelts
   like old rugs, it's them and
not them, same as when they move
   indoors, and stomp upstairs
as if a clogdance was a requirement
   for the job. But watch how they
hurl themselves joyfully out
   the window, bounce to their feet,
dust off, grunt, rush off
   through the goldenrod heading
straight for Ursa Major or Minor
   where they will look down
laughing, knowing we think they're there
   because we put them there.

Balance

With eyes equal to the dam he's built
incorporating willows, silt
& mud, a rusted pot, trees
bit off at equal heights, he glints,
circling lodge & dam, as apple-trees
slip into the water like old ladies
up to their ankles, then their knees.
Back from the brink, he's placed
large stones around the dam's bowed interlace
to hold it there, balanced by what
it lets go.

The Chef

He makes a racket as if sawing the dark
   into bite-size pieces. He says
if you stay still you rust. He thinks
   the truth happens in stages, you
taste it and move on. He is ripping
   something up on the table. He says
you must find your own hand. He picks up
   an egg he calls perfection without hair,
and rides it as it gallops in a number
   of directions, till he creates an appetite
for feathers and falls off bored.
   He says razorblades in the stomach
unlock appetites for razorblades.
   This is the real challenge, so he rambles
and howls across borders, getting away
   completely from comfortable corners
of pockets. He flushes out eagles,
   with his own hand strangles one,
strips it to the bone, pins it against
   a plate blue as the empty sky.

Lines

In the window-screen's grid I plot the young buck
who's blazed a line of maple saplings
so they gleam from each to each,
invisible passageways he's seen & grasped, thrashing them
out of air, rubbing as if his life depended on it,
& I go out, follow paths that follow no discernable reason
but are trodden deeper into the thatch down to red soil
& stone, crossing & recrossing, while chickadees weave courses
& tales over grids of old walls mink & chipmunk made tracks on,
& I move with them all, but after the fact, following
what they've left, even the stitch & darn of vanished insects,
acute angles and intersections of swallows,
& though they say the mind is no computer
& no mere binary mesh, I locate myself along lines laid down
long before my time.

iii
Carmen Miranda's Hat

A Dream of the Prehistoric

They come out dry, stretch & sing,
Let's see, chestnuts, yours and mine,
then divide & share them like crowns.
God knows they know gods. Scents
are a shade they sit under, while
a wolf gets used to their whistling.
In the hut made of, what, mastodon
tusks, reindeer antlers, branches & trunks?
they keep getting bigger. The baby
wrapped in skins & poppies is stretched
on a slate, while his older brother is
already turning to bearded pony, wisent,
bird on a stick, salmon swimming upstream
criss-crossed with moon marks.
Everyone dreams, & the threads are used
for everything they wear, or, decomposed,
the physical moment itself. A loud noise
could be thunder, or the sound that
turns them inside-out as they live
at the heart of echoes, everything touching,
and *see* means *understand,* and
understand means what it says.
But it's not so much the dream
they turn to or into; rather it's
the somewhere else that goes with them,
breaking open fire so it sticks
to the walls of caves as ochre hands
blown wide, & leading deeper from
space to space turning everything
into the lamp of a reason that's
dangerous as the tusk in the spine
or a landslide. Meanwhile, the bird-
headed man is numberless & disappears

in front of eyes that see him climb
like a lark up the tree whose rungs ring,
& see him return again & stay on the
flickering walls. He is the one who
wakens them into another dream where,
dazed by the everyday, everyone could
be everything & everything come down
out of the rock, out of the rock's
brown nipples, everything slippery to
the touch, & disembodied hands
grasp beginning & end at once, swimming
over each other. But then,
one day the bell rang, sun blared,
& survivors huddled together to tell
their stories & sing their songs in fits
& fragments. When I got there,
I just had time to find a few hand-puppets
& ivory carvings, figurines in coal,
before the authorities impounded my plane
& locked me up.

The Cow and the Wall

Up on former pastures cows once climbed & snorted
at something poking out at them, large trees now fly till they
run out of air, & the mountain itself tugs
out its roots, shedding bits of itself like bark
or hair caught on snags of a rough June sky.
But on the lower slopes cows still clamber about in fields
they keep clear with deer who lead them astray into corn-patches,
or, like the Holstein heifer Bailey, leap
over walls to get at fallen apples on my land,
where I watch her nip and slurp till they go off
in her four stomachs like timebombs quenched by pails
of gasoline so she takes off after herself
where she had last seen herself, trying to jump
back over the wall backwards & logical, again & again,
bellowing for me to put things back the way they were
when everything worked, turn things around
so she'll know what was where by what had been there.
Soon she's jumping backwards, expecting to go forward,
her rubber shoes hitting the flat stone keys,
accompanying herself in a low moan till the northern lights
go off in her eyes & the stones all round begin to
call out from their ancient deeps, an echo to her grand
confusion of mind, as if together they can solve
how place can stay the same yet reach
different conclusions until after a while it seems
as if the wall is wailing & the cow
jumping in place like a wall trying to clear itself,
growing less convinced it is making progress, going
from a place it no longer wants to a place
it can no longer reach & loving the world.

The Print

Sometimes I'm someone else, like—berserk.
I've been kicked off busses, bounced
from places I wouldn't be seen dead in,
and once left for dead in a Wal*Mart
parking lot. Tonight the house I'm paying off
is his, the air prickly & thunder still
on the prowl so my flesh crawls.
Sky's so close I could hook it &
drag it down to see what's there,
just like the bear last night who came
out of nowhere and pulled over the stump
I'd hauled from the woods last spring
to paint "Arthur & Ursula" on,
except now there's no Ursula.
Morning showed the rotted stump in shreds,
ants milling about in shock, their world
gone, some legless, some clamped
onto corpses, no idea which end was up,
nowhere home any more. Nothing else
was touched, not a leaf out of place,
as if to make a point, the only other sign
one flat footprint left carefully in the middle
of an old anthill at the side of the driveway
leading down and out but which
on closer inspection turned out to be my own.

The New World

He made the most of his mistake
in even being there. The music died,
the charm collapsed. They didn't
care for him, so he went home.
His voice was gone. He peeled off
his shirt, shaking out a dead bee.
He counted his heartbeats. A fly's buzz
briefly threw him off. Outside
the window a small plane crashed.
A stooped man staggered out
of the wreckage that blew up
behind him. I'd rather be a tree,
he thought, scratching the beebite.
He picked up his magic fork
and struck the corner of the table.
Everything quivered, then disappeared,
man, table, eventually fork. He took off
his clothes to reveal skin blue as sky.
Who needs wax and feathers, he said.
He took out his paints. He looked
in the mirror. He began to trace himself
in the glass until the facsimile
dropped off. But not before he'd stepped
right through it and out the other side.
Things got better immediately. This
is the new world, he said. You will find
everything here, and then some,
if you know where to look. There are
metaphors here we'd only dreamed about.
Nobody ever thought anyone could
make it here. How wrong they were.
I can give them great things if they
come over. We can all be as kings,
figuratively speaking.

Carmen Miranda's Hat

He peers out, parting the ferns. He is ready again
to love someone, perhaps construction workers,
perhaps ashcans and pigeoncoops on tar beaches,
if he can find them. He walks through shale & granite,
between, on one side, a swamp with big things in it,
& on the other a sandbank along which treads a silky path
leading to a few rows of corn & ginkgo trees with fruit
that sits on the ground like vomit & a mushy spring
feeding a stream with trout quick as laughter &
a coke bottle tinkering with the sun so he
has to put his hand across his striped face to shade
his painted eyes to see whatever might come through
the sandhills that squeeze the wind so it starts at him
like a flint-head. Now he knows who has passed that way,
urinating in the stream, scratching names on trees,
& who might well again in the foulness of time,
splashing ashore like lost seals, waving cloth & iron pots.
Give me your skins. He moves forward slowly
on what could have been feet, breathes hard, redoubles
his efforts, pushes through scrubby sumac, stubbing his toes
on dumb turtles, the smell of clean sand still in his nostrils.
He wants to tell them Good news, say You are welcome, welcome,
& share again the bounty on Carmen Miranda's hat, pass it around,
tropical, exotic. Here, eat my hat, eat my clothes,
sure, eat my skin, eat me. But they are not there,
maybe never were, unless, he thinks, they are lost somewhere
wandering about like marshgas, disappearing like bullfrogs
into their own harsh voices that never could sing &
their eyes may still be out there, though they cannot see me,
wanting me to find them, afraid as they wonder
how anything can be so still & empty, so quiet,
not even the tremor on a twig, as they race through space,
hair slicked back, white-knuckled, hanging on, not knowing

where they're headed. He pities them, but now he's alone
feels again the dew-claw beginning to push through his skin,
hears the whine and whisper of stars sleeping like bears,
gets scents from folds in the wind, time rotting in the breeze
coming from the great river's front door. This was
the world they'd wanted; they'd also wanted its opposite.
What they took crumbled. Now he sits on what remains
of a rock they made in a place they'd created to look
as natural as possible, even burying in the process
one of their own villages to make a great meadow,
& he watches the huge screen, his eyes projecting all
they can imagine & all they know, & then some, for where
they were concerned there was always the improbable
if not the impossible & he has to leave room for that
& the unimaginable for they were big on the unimaginable,
& as he watches he goes around tasting flowers again,
native & foreign-born the same to the tongue that had tasted
macaw & elephant, camel & tiger, giant sloth & mastodon, and,
in truth, had tasted a few of them from time to time—bitter, bitter.
He practices the few words they taught him & he remembers
because you never know. Yes, he says, you are welcome to my hat.
It is a nice hat, always in season & it will feed you for ever
if you sing & wear it properly. For it is the goddess
Carmen Miranda's hat, on loan. She's going to want it back.

Bucolic

—et in Arcadia ego

The wait of a child, a curse, a yell,
  and an owl, at noon. A wide shadow
crosses the lawn. Such are my days,
  and at night trumpets and guitars,
and a thump thump thump of
  electric bass. But tonight, just
as I'm falling asleep, out back they set off
  fireworks. They're having a good time.
I'm choking on burnt tires, charred flesh.
  I stumble over and rap on their door.
Stop the damn noise! No one answers
  though their laughter does die down
a bit, and a child screams. Then it all
  starts up again and a Roman candle
flares, a rocket, a ratchet of Chinese
  firecrackers and then explosions with
enough force to bring down hills.
  I slink back. It seems hours, but
eventually, head under pillow, I do
  fall off the edge into sleep. After a while,
I'm woken by the silence. The child is quiet
  and the other hooligans must be sodden
on the kitchen floor or passed out on
  their barbecue or fallen into the goldfish pond
they stock and the mink empties. I get up
  and go out. In the dark, in the silence,
stars popping overhead and a satellite or two
  close as fireflies, I stand on the deck.
Mountains are sensed not seen, presences
  that press in. Yes, this is the time to
sort out the universe. But I might as well
  be asleep. Nothing comes, and the silence

is a bit unnerving, and especially this blackness.
  I stare out and wait for it to pass.
It doesn't, and bed seems lonely. So I think
  of setting their place on fire and blaming
a stray rocket. I get so caught up I almost
  fall over the railings into the bushes where
it might take weeks or even months for someone
  to find me, and when they do, *Who's that?*
they'll say. And no one will know, except
  the child who says, He came over on July 4,
and told us to stop. We pretended not to hear him.
  Then he went away. Who pushed him?

iv
THE WEATHERMAN

The Mirroring

They put up steel. Take
it down. Glass, one minute up,
the next in pieces.
On a dark blue day with
the content of the sea sweeping
through, crying, one minute
it's there, the next not.
Sky's a blank to torture &
drop. When I was young
it seemed answerable. Now
it's level when you look at it
but when you look away it's
folds & pleats you can get
lost in, & if you crawl inside
it has all the appeal of a root-
cellar. But where are the roots?

I stand in the light of our high
back field among wild thyme whose
purple scent knocks you off your feet,
heat rising from rocks no one could move
into walls, & I'm all cracked up, looking
off rocks into blue up down around,
at my feet, far as the eye can see,
& I make a cloud St. Theresa in
ecstasy, the mind turning in on
itself, which is to say out, going
out, breaking up & in each part
& in the breaking a new up
& down, in & out, far & near all
strung together & along by something
like birdsong, something like wind
inside that song that bends notes

like light for as much as it can take
& then mirrors itself with you in the middle
doing much of the mirroring.

The Weatherman

"A distant cloud, a thunder-bud—it grew...."
—Hart Crane, "Powhatan's Daughter"

1

Nothing goes away. We pick and choose,
  rip and run, or stay. In cellars, each house
betrays its meaning. Air upsupported
  drops. In the darkness, we first
hear bells, like showers. And we are
  happy enough. Then puzzlement moves
back in on itself so quiet we almost
  can't tell if the city on the hill's
shirt or flame, a swirl of flies on
  Chinese silk, or just the land
riding off in electric night,
  sillion and sheen.

2

We say now we're alive, free as roots
  that spread as if there were no other place.
What was motion's now a name or thing.
  Our black beads knock together,
the same crowd we came with,
  and we watch and call a show the stranger
who holds a snake that tangles in her hair
  and coils her waist. Its loose strands hang.
Her hands are a heritance we'll pay for,
  the dusky body—but not yet.

3

In the garden something decays at what
   should be deflected or reflected,
re- or disappear. If rape's on trial this
   is some mess. Quicklime is stealthy,
and spreads with applause over a variety
   of accounts, some figurative, some
payable, some not.

4

   What isn't pinned down flies off
to another world like this, while here
   the natural no longer represents the fullness
of the natural. The visitors find this funny
   as they pore over blueprints whose scintillations
whip up winds. If all this sounds a bit strange
   to them it's strangely close to home,
which is probably why it never can be home,
   especially to the weatherman whose weather
this is, but who says he's not responsible
   for it, he's just telling it like it is and
has to be. Nobody's to blame.

Canon 501

The song was moist, filing away,
  drifting while we drifted, something
in blackface, Al Jolson of birdland,
  not quite right, prophesizing until hoarse
who knows what. The locals say he
  draws poison from you, *angatkuk,*
shaman, though they don't believe it.
  Then the incongruous smell of
chrysanthemum crossed us up and
  we remembered the service-station
with someone in handcuffs. Probably
  a mistake, said the attendant, though
they do get violent. The prisoner yawned.
  Our map lumbered from point to point
as if trying to remember something itself,
  anything. We tossed it and got out.
On the long walk back the tundra looked cozier
  by moonlight, everywhere the same,
white as bleached whalebone. But
  things had not been right all day.
In the damp heat everything was wobbly,
  even the bride at the old mission who
seemed to grow clouds like companions,
  drawing them after. I glimpsed a ring
of seal-fur flash on her wrist. *Mm-hmm,*
  unh-hunh they went. The honeymoon
was spent beyond the rigs. It was enough
  for them it didn't rain or snow though
the driftwood fire they made beside the boats
  was all smoke. The sea sounded obscure
as if it had no shape and was empty.
  We tried to capture it on Canon 501
and sent it south, but even that seemed staged.

Aleut Reverie

Beyond the other lights, a stumbling
  bodiless light, and then from white water
whiter water, and a brighter light.
  There isn't much to tell me what it is
from these high cliffs where from time
  to time I've stumbled over old green
skulls or weathered bones. The spray
  flies up and I duck, as I used to under
the camera's black cloth to see the land
  and ocean tossing in the sleep of
the Moon's sister as she looked down
  on young men in kayaks, wood visors
prickly with sea-lion whiskers blowing out
  like wisps of smoke as they paddled past
the Evening Star, past Bundles-of-Codfish
  and the Caribou, heading away, away....
And I head back, turning away from the
  light on the sea that's now flickered
out, back toward the sound of one
  hesitant drum almost drowned
in a radio's slow drone.

The Island

"Be not afeared; the isle is full of noises"

Pulling away from land, the river sucks and sobs.
Undercut banks and shoals hover above the receding tide,
collapse. Through soggy stogies "Cyrus" yessirs me.
Yessir, that's right. Yessir to anything I say,
answering almost in the abstract, still,
after weeks, keeping me out. Circles
of his Gullah slide over the few words
of Al and Bill, his sons, sink under water
tawny as deer pelts. Then everything goes quiet
as long stretches of marsh picked over by egrets.
Lead weights take their lines down fast. Circles
link, then split. I toss a pebble in that
strikes its own note till one of theirs quietens it.
I shiver, and join their silence, warm and black
as the mud from which from time to time they draw
out Queenie's catfish, eels whose snakeheads they crush
with axe or heel, then slop into buckets with yellowtails,
darkening as they swell, eyes blueing over.
Cyrus lands a stingray, *devilfish* he calls it.
As he plants a large unclean sneaker on its pasty
underside where human lips smack and suck
in a white face his cataract stands out,
full-moon. He hacks the tail off with a rusty pocketknife;
a bleeding finger-stump is all that's left.
He cuts his hook out from a wing, and gently
toes the stingray back. It rises, lips moving
as if about to speak, then sinks.

—

He's lived here all his life, though no one knows
his age or name, or just won't tell me. Only the women

have names. Each day on the pier, not far from
the plantation house, off the road overhung
with palmettos and live oaks pulsing with boat-tailed
grackles, I've sat and watched him fish, waiting.
Over the weeks, I've given him cigars.
But the only time he'd looked at me was when
he snagged a long-lost crab-cage. Grabbing the rotting
rope, he slipped a knot through deck-boards so
the crabpot hung, pouring black silt through
its bars, emptying its empty self. He laughed,
startling me. I heard my father's voice:
I like them fine. I understand the nigger.
Just remember they're like children. A happy race.
They'd laugh even if their backsides were on fire.
But never trust one. "They sure can put a biting
on you," Cyrus said, slapping. Light,
cut from paper strips, blew over the water,
unable to penetrate. "Yessir."

When things get too bad, you should take a certain opportunity, when for instance he is with the Driver in the provision room, and you at the door, with a rope in your own pocket, then pull it out and.....

—

Slowly, he begins to talk, and I begin to hear
through the Gullah. His voice emerges from
the haze of smoke until one day, invited
to his place, I get there early: a tabby-cabin,
slave-built, thick walls, whitewashed, of cemented
rock and shell, red corrugated roof, beside
the massive iron tub once used to boil
indigo seeds, but now a trap for rain.

I have had the negroe houses all white washed outside and in which I am in hopes will add to their health. There is no more sickness than we would expect. The worst is pregnant women. Negroes are too valuable to run any risk to their health, and pneimonia is awful.

I'd passed this cabin on the walks I took, sticking
to the paths of Indian midden-shell and sand
that kept me above the terrifying swamps,
every kind of poison snake, gators, and fears beyond.
"Would you care to take some lemonade?"
We're on his porch. Piglets, some reverted
to wild boar, root among the chickens just
below. A turkey-vulture circles over
slash-pine in the swamp. A dog that seems
a cross between a mastiff and wild boar
lies at my feet. I shake my head. No thanks.
Not yet. Cyrus sucks a stogie. "In them
old days," he says, "when Mrs. Weston's father
owned the land, the place was thick with boars.
Just choose your pig and shoot it. I used to run
them down on foot, the China pigs with their
short legs. We'd smoke and cure the hams, make
bacon, chitterlings." He shakes his head.
The pig-dog stirs.... *There is an old plantation saying which we can*
see everyday, viz.: A Negro never knows when he is welloff.
Coon hunts with hounds in packs of two, three
hundred, maybe more. And in them days
the isle was fat with springs, freshwater springs
so full we had to cap them fast to stop
the isle from drowning. And when a spring was struck
it spouted in the air at least ten feet..
freshwater ponds as big as lakes—and fish—
but now the akafer's all broke...it's that
mainland development...." He stops, and looks
across the sandy road where Mrs. Weston's
'Starman', the ancient Apaloosa no one
dares approach, stands with streaks of thick
dry blood around his fetlocks and half-way up
his legs. Flies pester. He's in a foot-deep trench
he's worn along a fence that keeps him from
a mare. He paces one way along it, then
comes trotting back. Cyrus rises, picks up

a can that smells like pine-tar, and a dirty rag.
He crosses the road, pushes through the gate.
Starman watches, then steps out of the pit,
nickering. He stands stock-still while Cyrus daubs
his legs, talking all the while to the horse
who opens his nostrils wide, breathing Cyrus in.
Back on the porch, he uses the same rag
to dab his pearly eye. "If I may,
I'll trouble you now for that lemonade." I use
the language carefully, as if it weren't
my own. I sip and listen. *The myrtle has grown some, but not a great deal. One of the Pitisporum is dead, the other looking well. Old Daniel is in the ricefield. We are well.*
"There was a little girl that used to hang around
at Middle Place. I warned her not to pick up
pretty things, but then one day she saw
a little rattler, and picked it up.... That night
I slept in a cabin mostly woodcutters used.
I woke in the early hours. A hand had grasped
my wrist. A strong black hand. I pulled, but couldn't
move. 'Why then,' I thought, 'if you got me
I'm gonna get you!' So I grabbed this hand with my
free hand. He pulled. I pulled. We wrastled there
together and fell down on the floor like fighting dogs.
He pulled on me, drug me toward the door
until he throwed me off, like he's disgusted,
and vanished through the floor. As I lay there,
fair wore out, I saw my whole left side
where he had grabbed my flesh shook and quivered,
all its strength gone. But yet I paid no mind,
and pushed against the door and went outside
to look about. No one there. A small part
of the moon was visible, and that was all.
So I went back inside and saw that he'd
returned and thrown the bed about so it lay
upside-down. I put the room to rights

and lay back down, and soon was sound asleep.
Next morning in the cookshed a woman asked
if I was sick, and so I told her all.
'It's happened all before,' she said. 'Take salt
and strew it round the hut'. But I never did.
"And weren't you scared?" I asked. "Nosir, nosir.
I wasn't scared. Nothing there to scare.
It could have been a slave who tried to show me
something. He wanted me outside. And if
I hadn't fought he might have shown me something
could have changed my life. Lots of slaves killed
here in old plantation days. Each got a story.
Many a time I seen them, heard them, like
the land speak—and I ain't the only one.
One walk by here, right here, in front of Queenie's
house." I glance across to Queenie's tabby-cabin,
Queenie, regal as her name, Indian
copper cheekbones, who liked an evening nip
and sang loud as she walked: Don't care where
you throw me/ Since my Jesus own me.... You can
beat and bang me—Jesus save me. Lord,
touch our bodies.

London was drowned on Monday morning about 9 ocl. The cause...Thomas deserved punishment...taken to barn...his reply was he would drown himself before whip him.... My orders have been no one is to touch the corpse, and will remain if not taken at the next tide.... Numerous instances of ingratitude evinced in the African character.... Not to be trusted.... 'Lincoln'....

"Another time, at dusk, I took the track
that lay beside a burial place for slaves
and Guales before that—for this was all
Creek Mary's. Right there my old black mule stop
dead in his tracks. He balks and trembles though
I gives him a cut or two with my old switch.
Finally, with slaps and curses I make him move.
But he seem in a daze. When I gets home
I tells them what had happened. 'Something spook him,'
they say. 'Gator, mebbe. Next time it happen

and he don't move just light a match and stick it
by his nose.' So next day at sun-fall, same thing.
So I gets down and walks to that mule's head.
I strikes the match—and scarce had time to get back
in the cart when that ol' mule take off. He shoot ahead,
and as he get up steam—a black shape up ahead
crawl like a cat out of the swamp, and two
black paws or hands the size of dinner plates
spreads out. I recognized those hands. They raise
as if to get me stop, and I would have too
but that ol' mule run like the wind, tail up.
Maybes he needed to tell me something, something
I need to know, and maybes would have spoke....
There's some, some in the swamps, each a story."

—

At summer's end, I'm walking through thickets
of the yupon that gave this isle its name:
Place-of-the-Yupon-Berries, source of the Creek
"black drink," purgative and purifier.
I find myself among a herd of tiny
island deer, and walk among them, as in
a dream, touch their tawny backs, color of mud.
The tide moves out against the wind, then turns
against itself. The moon comes up, casting
my shadow on the deer; they move on. I drift
among them into places not there by day. Palmettos
rasp, gnats catch in my hair. The herd wanders
to the edges of the swamp and I walk into
the shadowed hummocked marsh, into a vaulted room
prickly with planets, listening.

v

The Power of the Name

Post-Industrial

The old slopes flap like muslin.
   Snow gleams as if angels were
reinventing themselves as snow.
   These mountains point to themselves
as if they were photos so you'll know
   they're really there. At their foot,
flashes like a fire going out above
   the railway bridge that hasn't
seen a train in decades. The bent rails
   are their own cargo they carry
from nowhere to nowhere else.
   Yet even from here you can hear
the wind strumming rusted struts.
   In day's deep grain sounds scrape by,
steel-ribbed, all spirit. The bridge is
   now a model of itself moving on staves
to the unsteady beat of invisible valves,
   driving into the horizon and down
the other side where there are no
   narrow ways, just damp grass and
a sky that smells of pitch, going all ways
   at once without the burden of direction.

Our Town

1

Our children braid their hair. Each
   has several skins, they think, so
nothing matters, though when the epidermis
   tears like silk they'll realize they're
silhouettes, frost on a burning roof.

2

   Floorboards shake a bit. Someone
reaches for a flower. Birds burst and
   fish squirm. Once God was a heft.
Now between worlds sparrows
   squeeze through winters. Nothing
will be decided. There are resemblances
   and resemblances, that's all,
and we are separated from both.

3

   The perfume of woodpulp is spreading
 and can sicken. Under its weight
    more children leave. It is late now.
The shadows are deserting. A pigeon
    is pacing on a sill, on the one
dry spot. This is a small town.
   You can hear the dough rising next door.

Ghosts

In this kind of night the fugitive
is forgiven and the others flock before us
in molefur back to the jail where
they gave birth, and from which
we stretch out with them from town
to town, crude and undigested,
looking for ourselves who don't exist,
perhaps, except as a brief excitement
in another's eyes, a doubt in our own,
brief bloom of mind that functions
as whatever we are. If we exist,
it is as spies on ourselves with
borrowed eyes, walking attics pierced
from time to time by a ray crammed
with motes going in many directions
at once in a kind of buffoonery,
and in their tracks we're forced to make
patterns like constellations, naming them
brief as flowers, and so the broken wheel
keeps churning, figments feel and
fragments float into the exhaustion
of systems that sing, evasive as air,
there till we stop looking, then not.

The Haunting

Sky's edge is cast-iron, its sharp brim
and long lines. Winds blow through grasses
but eggs are unbroken. We're safe, even if
in the park the talk is of prisoners, now loose
state-wide. Underfoot glass sparkles, like heaven's
broken dome, and at the back of all this
is a kind of haunting, someone entering
in black shoes, hopping holes, dodging
pillars. Thunder wheels. Here the city's
network crowds and shrinks to a sandgrain
about to bloom and cover the sky with
its own brightness, blotting out those
imaginings we call constellations and go
into space, shadowing the moon,
leaving tracks we might again call
constellations that will point the same way
of no direction for ever then drift out
into the blackness where you'd think
there was intense heat and light, the sun
being there, but which is in fact darker
than anything in the word black and yet
somehow something that is like light
and gives off something we can account for
and which might account for us, and it
curves and splays with lines & forces
on a beach with no sea, and a horizon
that lifts to let you look under and there
you see something old and familiar that
scares you since you saw it as a child
waking alone in a large bed facing a wall-length
mirror in which whatever it was being reflected
wasn't you or the room but something from
before words could say what it was, something

like the body itself, inarticulate and deep,
its black space, and it knew you for where you were,
and what, and where you were going.
But you didn't know it, and it went on and on
through you before you could gather it
and its monstrous cry into the shining ball of words
you were working on and, sobbing, sleep.

Pedagogical

It rained all week, but the ground's dry.
  I wake and dress. On the far side of the house
a backhoe coughs into life. Summer's short here.
  One sweep of the ax and it's gone, back into stars
that clip these hills with cold edges. These first fall nights
  something is pushing over stones big as tables,
tossing them about, turning walls and paths primeval.
  When asked, I am full of theories, this and that,
probably that. And let it go. This morning, crossing
  the street, our one street, run-down Victorian houses
with porches fuller than the rooms, I make out
  a blue haze brimming from the graveyard.
But after grabbing a bite at Boomagoo's Eatery
  I'm ready for anything. When I enter the classroom,
for once my students seem ready, or at least they're quiet.
  So I take a risk, and talk about poetry. I get
carried away, telling them how a poem floats,
  and opens its mouth, how poetry is an animal
and turns everything animal, gives everything breath,
  and fills it with rhythms like our own. I write one
on the board and tell them it's about a place like this
  by someone who lives in a place very much like this.
I read it out, twice, then, turning back to them,
  repeat it by heart. For once, they are listening.
And watch as I take the poem down, lay it on the stream
  now in full spate at the foot of the desk, float it
off like a leaf or curled bark, and we all see it flash and
  turn and dive in bright water stained with run-off
from the parking lot and the last dairy-farm left,
  heading for the river, which we can now hear
as if for the very first time.

The Theory of Evolution

There was morning, ashes not yet stirred,
loosening smoke in chimneys and motion
in windows.
                        The air glittered, an arc.
What am I then, today, when my bones
end in clouds and the quiet of wings
falls over the path so I am brushed out,
and when the sun passes up and over
I am disappeared?
                                  Twenty years ago
I didn't know it spun so fast. But
things die. My students look at me
expecting to hear something else.
After all, myth centers on immortality,
and out the window we can see animals
whose provisions spill out of the seasons,
out of the spreading sunlight
by now incredible, complete in itself,
roots wide as marble, its shock coming off
the river as it happens.
                                    But mouths are
everywhere. Soon horizons stack up,
everything peels back to show what's really there,
the mesh of flesh holding it all together
until everything comes breaking from its shadows.
Then beasts grab as much as they can and in the wind
quickly turn inside-out or make slower transitions
that look random but in fact are only
as random as flames, as free as shadows.

Snow

It is no symbol. It is
   white, just white.
As it falls it is just
   itself. It is no reflection,
it is no color. It is
   the same before it fell
and after. It could be innocent
   but that means it's
nothing, and it's not nothing.
   Nor is it suggestive of
chastity, purity etc. Or
   shouldn't be. It is not
even itself, for we have
   been told exactly what
that is, really, and it is
   not that. It can be nearer
than near or farther than far,
   it makes no difference. It's
in our face but cannot reflect us.
   We are not it. If you say
it has a purpose you're
   talking about yourself or
something else. I say it is
   satisfactory for what it is.
I'd even say you could say
   it's friendly or lovely until
you get lost in it, and then it is
   selfless, without self,
just like you
   becoming it.

Translation

By the rising path stones are piled,
one on one in a descending scale
till the top pebble is tiny and precarious.
Under a moon in monotone some stream
still runs, but the pond has turned
to ice. It is climbing painfully out
of itself, rising in cymbals over
its banks. The meadow is white.
The young pines with windchimes is silent
till snow starts to fall again, becoming
six clear notes in almost endless variation.

Telephone Wires

At night they sail like comet tails.
  By day their cup runs over and they yearn
for darkness. How different a picture is by night.
  In the midst of life they can think about
your death. You, in the same circumstances,
  might think about theirs. They travel
lightly in an incomprehensible world
  while leaves change and light turns.
They could be gods savoring their own beauty.
  Nothing can humiliate them, nothing offend.
They touch and touch, press close, stretch out,
  press in, strong and sturdy as trumpets,
close and quiet as mirrors, never completely
  themselves yet serene as labyrinths, balanced
and aligned into other worlds, leaping intervals
  like music, a dreaming that dreams it can
be anyone, cure or cause anything. Nothing
  weighs them down with what they know
for they remember nothing. At best, it's all nostalgia,
  the amnesia of shadows. A million angels
perch on each strand of wire and the sky takes
  their shape sailing on and on where it holds us
in the mesh of its rigging, and there we hope to hang
  on a sea that never bubbles or bursts until
we have to float down saturated into furniture
  squatting like repressed violence. They don't love us.
We are always demanding, too late or too early,
  never exact. In their halls are echoes of
moonless nights turning inward, cinders
  of addresses. It is cold. It is lonely. So they march,
vivid in the landscape, striding up and down,
  gobbling up everything, cars and saints,
babies and Dostoevsky, in a loopy catalepsy,
  lost in an unending spirit of revelation.

Millennium

Wind, dry sticks from which
light is born wearing its skin
inside-out along a riverbank
& in scoured streambeds where stones
are still unspent, getting into
their stride, grinding on in flashes
while day flows trying to make
the world last but hills behind me
hunker down like something in the mind,
& shapes on the water are more rumors
the dead trees give off, giving it up
in a language of shadow, while
the century breaks overhead
like a blank stare, & suddenly
I see a boy I thought a rock
take his mallet & smash the ice so bits
break off & flow downstream,
& he runs laughing, &
an old man I hadn't noticed leaps up
like a startled chicken & starts painfully
to cross the field as if he's missed or
is late for something important,
little snowdevils spinning all round him
like prayerwheels until at once they stop,
& he stops too, looking around as if
for the first time at embers
of whiteness, hills, the soundless sky,
what cannot be caught & what
cannot quite be believed in.

Someone

1

Water in stars arranges itself
to shine wildly. I look out,
then plunge into trackless dark
that's monument to the glare of silence.

2

Someone is walking beside me,
more than shadow, chest filled
with dark flowers. Snow dances
in starlight.

3

I praise the persistent little waters
that move alone, focused
as mind in which the neocortex of stars
continually reinvents itself,
expanding itself even into local air.

Everything

In water space changes and
  is empty, on and on. In water
the doors are down, everything crumbles,
  flowing both closer and farther away.
There's no need to question. Everything begins
  when everything seems, like the image
thrown on the blank wall. When the singing
  starts blue spreads into sky, and what was
unheard unsecured becomes secure. Everything
  becomes clearer like everything else. Pools
catch the scent of mind; their fire has
  dimensions. Now everything is pure event,
delicious. Now gods are self-encountering,
  recognizing themselves in the way everything
flows to underwater flowering which is
  the water formalized, so if everything
is born in slavery, it embraces it and
  it's free, burning into the world the picture
of the world, everything reflecting
  everything else, and is that thing,
irreducible, back and forth.

Story

"I am a salmon in a river"

—*The Book of Amergin*

Deep in the water, a far light,
an extreme of light, a glare of snow
fresh from its source as the heart
stirs night's gravel, picking up
speed, distance giving way, blurred
by gleams that leap, taking on
forms, taking something
for granted, singing with no sound,
breathing together air covered
with glass on cold gravel,
shapes shifting, taking rhythm
from what's offered, flexing
to another proximity, famished
& ragged with what they
have left, untangling themselves
as they aim for the doors
& a room where a storybook
lies open at a page all exultation
& unmoored shadows, climbing
out of the glass into silk, scattering
scales onto galaxies, abstract
space that exactly mirrors
the brightness they have leapt
right out of themselves.

Wind

through bluestone walls steadied
by skims & chinks, the wind,
divider & joiner, bringing in what
was far away, clarifying & confusing,
wind, the first idea, impulse
informing all flesh & non-flesh
that makes it leap out of background
decay & stasis, spirit, inspiration, breath,
so once here it seems to come
from inside & call the outside,
calling it back, & the outside
replies, calling it in.

Seed

from inside the steel box a white arm
reaches round, fingers fumbling for the bolts, someone
inside squirming like a magician to slip straps,
strip down to a different surrender that once free
will push like freight through margins & floes, pry sod & air
so the holes will not close, insisting into existence, pushing
down dream to draw on, suck it up into gold & going,
lamps fastened to hip & head to skewer
litheness on the pulse, shock itself into rain, past pebble
& worm, nerves dancing, fingers flung at moon & sun, toes dug
into embers, light slowly whirling in & through, a cadence linked
to birdsong that never falters & finds itself in itself
scattering from the brow hard black songs, bright trills
that fall & sit, waiting for new arms to reach,
fingers to loosen fountains
day & night, make almost anything,
naked clear & preemptive

Desert Sky

Clouds forming in a swirl round Jupiter
as dark settles in, a whirlpool spinning out
something as I look up, which feels the same
as looking down and in, and somewhere out there,
as in a fortune-teller's globe, something
coming together where the visible is inscribed
on the invisible, inner and outer shape one another,
and I am the desire in the middle,
when all the birds of day are silent
and the wind has sucked remnant light
from the deepest parts of trees so it hovers
with a broken shudder until it too
is swept up and away into the eyes of moths,
cells of stones, while dark floods in,
taking its place, revealing more night and
night itself, clear or cluttering, revealing
or revealed, calling down, calling up, to the
sharpest pinch of distant light concentrated
in the star's mind, quiet in the center
of the whirlpool spinning, grinding out
more stars and the light that will grow
and pour in behind the dark, the light
that is dark, pouring inward.

St. Theresa Says

I am fire & plucked chicken, both,
footprints on a dry riverbed, shadows on the bank.
I am brown hands flapping in a monsoon, shipwrecked near
Dido's palace & a Coca Cola stand. In my pocket is a poem
by Pierre Reverdy I was learning by heart until
the director said *cut.* I am Tollund man who died
in joy, strangled, his mind a kind of honey,
his stomach sprouting grains. I am a young girl's
scented letter to the world. I am that girl's legs
jiggling under her desk, her pen describing what
she has not yet known, while in the distance
presents are being unwrapped & flowers sparkle like eels
in shallows. I am that distance blown up to show
lemon trees filtering something from the air &
returning it to darkness like a gift. I am proud as charity;
dreaming of a love taking hold like a sailor's song.
But flesh is a shade I only sit in, naked, by a low fire,
while a consoling star traces a blue mark down
my chest, & onto my thigh, a shadow like a reed.
One wavering line circles my breasts, & falls
down my back like water. There's a bite mark
on my lip, & another on my hand. God alone suffices.

The Necessary Angel

—*World Trade Center, September 11, 2001*

She stands atop a heap that smokes and shifts.
What looks like rigor is a backward look
as she turns her head. Below her, wings
and little feet, feathers and sharp edges,
mouseparts, cogs and wheels of old machines,
a flower, a hand sans fingers, things sans
everything. Peering past her wing-edge she has
no sense of depth as the deep gray swirls behind
and all around. She has no fingers. Her hands
are stumps. What she'd once grasped now falls away,
lying all around. If she could make a tear her eyes would fill
and not know where she was. She tries to rise
from slag but her feet are no bird's that can grasp
and release, grip and go. They are more a mermaid's,
flowing deeper and blacker into the rock, spreading out like a seam,
holding her precariously in place. Her wings
are stiff. She holds them out like torn parchment
no one can yet read. Beauty burns
and the angel with it in a slow heatless flame.
But she keeps her pose, straining upward. Slowly turning back
to face the wind, she feels in the depths
something moving, struggling upward, making wings.

We Two

I follow the poem. I have no choice.
He has me in his mouth. I can't see
where we're going but as we travel
from place to place he drops me off.
There is something to be had in each
but I am shy. The poem is not. He can go
anywhere, even under girls' skirts
like a fantasy come true, the invisible man,
nothing of him showing but some
accoutrement like a cigar or pipe,
before that too fades into adventurous air.
He's a constant shift, visiting places
that weren't there before him.
I am often happy. I can rub my hands
and up I'll pop out of the bottle.
Where are we going today, master?
I say. It's all a bit tiring, but at night
I seldom sleep alone. The poem listens
and looks out for me, sometimes climbing
into my bed, the hugging and loving bed-fellow.
But he can be nasty too. You were nothing
before you met me, he'll say, relieving himself
on my shoe. He tells me secrets I could
never think of by myself. If he lies
how can I know? Let him lie. The poem
keeps to himself, plays close to the vest,
seldom goes all in, and when he thinks
I'm not listening he'll whisper, I am lonely,
lonely. But I am never more than
a few steps behind picking up his crumbs
and sometimes him. He's been known
to trip and fall. He doesn't like this. Thanks,
he grunts. Here, don't go away. I've got something

for you. I run over. Poof! Nothing, or a crackle
and a few black marks like those they find
when someone's spontaneously combusted.
I scoop them up. You never know.

Barn Burning

Like a red cypress towering over the gables, sparks fast stars,
  and the flames blowing upward, a madness, the insistent madness
that goes away briefly, dies down, drops down the far side,
  then comes back up refreshed to push out like a light into
the darkness and gives darkness a false depth, as if,
  if you ever went far enough it would turn into something else
too bright to look at, something that shows you yourself
  as you really are, the other side of the way decades have
shaped up and shaped you, not the way you really are,
  not the way you are now, as if you could pull on a new skin,
jubilant and sweet-smelling. Pines sway in the gusts the flames make,
  not the wind. The barn roof's intwisted, caught up,
and little white flames run up and down the long spine
  like flashing water too cool to do any damage. An old barn,
newly gutted and rebuilt, almost done, almost a new thing,
  if that's possible, or the filled-in frame of a desire starting
from the roof, then the sides. Now the tiles are falling down
  the flanks and the flanks collapsing ribs into insides you can
only guess at, what was meant for what, what did what,
  how it worked. But there's a logic here, a shape of destruction
you could figure out, given the context, and though the dry grass
  all round is catching and going off in all sorts of directions
so the mind cannot take it all in, even against the breeze
  fed by the fire, going to where it wants, without forethought,
spitting great gobs with the gusts fire itself is creating,
  and now it is all involved, and no one coming to put it out
this far in, miles from anywhere, and I am the only watcher.
  I watch. I could use the phone but it's down. So
I watch and wait to see what will happen I couldn't predict,
  see if when it all collapses there is relief in the air, if things
go on as before, if anyone notices, if there is anything left
  to relate to, anything that survived to be built on from the
ground up, or if it is too late and what I'd watched was all

there was, just a burning down, or if what was there is still there,
a shape etched into night, a spectral afterimage, its contour
clear as it had been before, so you can close one eye and trace it
with a finger, blurring the sharp edges, pitch of roof, where the wall
turns and points to the well-house and the rows of cypresses
once lining the driveway, and it will follow your finger, trailing
off it, moving where it moves, stopping when it stops until
you point and shake it off, still living, or drag its brilliant line
only you can draw over fields and sky, the line only you
can read, taking it all again to what it was but not where,
or there and somewhere else, when all I really wanted was
to have it nowhere, but nowhere's always somewhere and this thing
seems sworn to keep me, burning my outline around me,
consuming me, burning me up to go out in a plume of glory,
taken off somewhere, dispersed in a different form, broken down
into particles that scatter like bright seeds, like thoughts, fire
a knife replacing every part and organ with something shining,
not here but everywhere, going in at my eyeballs and ears,
deep into lungs that had dried to the skeleton of a leaf,
moving around inside until the features stand out against
the night sky like a jubilee, the flare of a single match.

How to Speak Welsh

> "He loved his cabin: there
> nothing happened."
> —Richard Hugo

Rain, gowned as a widow, night
black and bound fast. A beast
outside, silent. Being lost's
accomplishment. The wind
reflects night, drags across and
falls like a drunk over stones
and branches. I have tossed
my useless name, a past that
swerves by like this gale.
The walls, dimensions it takes
forever to reject I've replaced
with not much. One fly pings
my light and falls, again and again.
One light flickers on the mountain
opposite. I take down a How To
book. My shelves are full of them,
How To Speak Welsh. I have
nothing to hide.

The Power of the Name

"These days which seem empty and fruitless"
—Rilke

Forget the western sky's steep steps.
Forget the law of the emplumada & risen god.
Just assume for yourself a name wide enough
in which sky can turn to its opposite yet
still feel like home, where dents & marks
work out to become prints like your own
you follow into a dark desert where bubbles
burst & the wind rushes ahead matching itself
against anything. Here you can take the sharp
cold light & train it on the shapeless sand
so it grows hooks & handles. So
in these days which once seemed nameless
empty & fruitless, you can now grow roots
between stones & drink from anywhere.

Scalemodel

"The mockingbird is imitating life"
— Randall Jarrell

For years the house was out of control,
 spitting like campfire sparks.
If I hid, it was to watch things closely;
 there was anger here. And then
one day, at the edge of the woods,
 a mockingbird mocked, bringing
everything down to size. As I listened
 to him calling like a comic deity,
another mocked him, shrinking him too,
 and I laughed. From this grew my collection
of toy seas, miniature gods, babies small
 as punctuation, and the rest. Broken down
and reassembled they still manage to do
 what is required for the most part,
imperfect as they are. On my trees pruned
 and unpruned hang all sorts of
intimate joys and disasters, everything
 undermined by its scale, so, for instance,
anger's a bell, grief a balloon and integrity
 a whistle. They all seem well-nourished,
how, no one really knows. Sometimes when
 they sleep their bodies shine. Each day
they wake to enjoy the sensation of pretense.
 I get down to their level and watch them
the same way as a kid I laid my head
 along the model track, daring the
quickly enormous black locomotive
 to round the curve and go straight
through my eye deep into my head.

Walking Across the Room

Our bodies are cast to think themselves everywhere,
relentless as air, sternward, to stars, bellying

in the dark, sumptuous even on stone where they're
just shadow, each moment a short scene, a shawl

of white water drifting in low through things
while the soul, incandescent, but as here as bread,

is a kind of billowing breaking up in flashes.
This way hearts break the better to support themselves.

In its shade we hear the murmur of shade, like birds rising
in fountains. The body is now complete. Naked,

I am introduced to myself, walk across the room
my steps lamps as, like a hawk, the dark

turns and swoops, making it hard still to breathe
on my own, but I breathe.

Metaphor

What I'd say is the wind, direct.
Or the wind waiting to say this. But instead
I'm speechless, as if the mouth had something
in it that shouldn't be there. And that's
what comes out. When I try to say what
I have to say out comes *antifreeze,*
knave of hearts, rupture, rapture, ruin.
I have said what I have to say
in so many roundabout ways I'm dizzy.
I keep saying it because nobody listens
and so nobody says stop. If they think
anything they think, That is what such
people do. They hide things. And it's true.
I do take refuge. If I'd been at war
I would say what happened to be believed.
I shot this one, that one shot me, we are all
empty husks. But what once might have been
shock has become ritual. So I open the till,
stick my hand in, pull out a fistful of small change,
hand it over. Here, this is another metaphor.
Spend it wisely. Say goodbye, and mean it.

About the Lena-Miles Wever Todd Poetry Series

The editors and directors of the Lena-Miles Wever Todd Poetry Series select one book of poems for publication by Pleiades Press and Winthrop University each year. All selections are made blind to authorship in an open competition for which any American poet is eligible.

Other Books in the Series

Motherhouse by Kathleen Jesme (selected by Thylias Moss)
Lure by Nils Michals (selected by Judy Jordan)
The Green Girls by John Blair (selected by Cornelius Eady)
A Sacrificial Zinc by Matthew Cooperman (selected by Susan Ludvigson)
The Light in Our Houses by Al Maginnes (selected by Betty Adcock)
Strange Wood by Kevin Prufer (selected by Andrea Hollander Budy)